Computer

The Bible

Learn From The Basics to Advanced of Python, C, C++, C#, HTML Coding, and Black Hat Hacking Step-by-Step IN NO TIME!

CyberPunk Architects

All rights reserved.

CyberPunk Architects

Copyright 2018 by CyberPunk Architects
All rights reserved.

The following book is reproduced below with the goal of providing information that is as accurate and reliable as possible. Regardless, purchasing this book can be seen as consent to the fact that both the publisher and the author of this book are in no way experts on the topics discussed within and that any recommendations or suggestions that are made herein are for entertainment purposes only. Professionals should be consulted as needed prior to undertaking any of the action endorsed herein.

This declaration is deemed fair and valid by both the American Bar Association and the Committee of Publishers Association and is legally binding throughout the United States.

Furthermore, the transmission, duplication or reproduction of any of the following work including specific information will be considered an illegal act irrespective of if it is done electronically or in print. This extends to creating a secondary or tertiary copy of the work or a recorded copy and is only allowed with an expressed written consent from the Publisher. All additional right reserved.

The information in the following pages is broadly considered to be a truthful and accurate account of facts, and as such any inattention, use or misuse of the information in question by the reader will render any resulting actions solely under their purview. There are no scenarios in which the publisher or the original author of this work can be in any fashion deemed liable for any hardship or damages that may befall them after undertaking information described herein.

Additionally, the information in the following pages is intended only for informational purposes and should thus be thought of as universal. As befitting its nature, it is presented without assurance regarding its prolonged validity or interim quality. Trademarks that are mentioned are done without written consent and can in no way be considered an endorsement from the trademark holder.

CyberPunk Architects

Table of Contents

Introduction 9
Part 1: The Guide to Ethical Hacking for Beginners 11
Chapter 1: Setting Up a Hacking Environment 12
Chapter 2: How to Work with a Linux Terminal for Your Hacking Needs 17
Chapter 3: How to Make Sure That You are Anonymous Online 25

    What is a VPN and how will it keep me hidden? 28
    Which VPN is the best one to use? 29
    Which email software is the best to remain hidden? 29

Chapter 4: Setting Up NMAP 33
Chapter 5: What are the Best Password Cracking Tools? 38

    Aircrack-ng 39
    Crowbar 39
    John the Ripper 40
    Medusa 40

Chapter 6: What is the DarkNet? 42
Chapter 7: How to do Wireless Hacking 45
Chapter 8: Basic Steps to Keep Yourself Safe from Other Hackers 50

    Always take caution about what is shared online 50
    Setting passwords that are strong and unique 51

Download the Password Manager Tool 51

How LittleSnitch can help 51

Remember that you need a good antivirus program. 52

If you use Flash, then it is time to stop. 53

Take the time to do a backup of all your files on a regular basis. 53

Part 2: Advanced Hacking Techniques 55

Chapter 9: The Top Cyber Security Threats Today 56

Ransomware 56

IoT Botnet traffic 58

Phishing and Whaling 59

Machine learning enabled attacks 60

Chapter 10: Laying Down the Ground Rules for Hacking 63

What is ethical hacking? 63

What constitutes ethical hacking? 64

How do I actually protect myself? 66

What are some of the ways that I can stay protected from cyber-attacks? 67

Consider hiring an expert to help 69

Chapter 11: The Procedures for Proper Cybersecurity 70

Doing a vulnerability assessment 72

Penetration testing 73

Web application assessment 74

Network architecture security assessment 74

Mobile device and application assessment 75

Information security management 76

Mobile device forensics 76

Network forensics 77

Web and internet forensics 77

Malware analysis and reverse engineering 78

Insider threat assessment 78

Things to consider when it comes to mobile device security 79

Chapter 12: Should I Change My IP? Things to Consider During Infrastructure Monitoring 82

Chapter 13: Methods and Techniques for Hacking Like a Professional 87

How to hack administrative passwords 87

How to hack a WhatsApp account 89

MAC Address spoofing: Doing it the hard way 90

Part 3: The More You Know: Learning How to Code with Several of the Best Programming Languages 92

Chapter 14: How to Code with C# 93

Getting started with the variables 93

What data types will I use in C# 95

Working on a code 99

Chapter 15: How to Code with C++ 102

Creating the Hello World Program 102
Comments in the code 104
The variables in C++ 104

Chapter 16: How to Code with Python 108

Variables in Python 108
How to assign values to the variables 109
Assigning multiple values to a variable 111
Some of the standard types of data 111
Strings 113
What are lists? 114
The importance of keywords in your code 115
Statements 116
Working with operators and operands 117

Chapter 17: How to Code with C 119

Writing out a dummy code in C 119
Working on your second code 122

Chapter 18: How to Code with JavaScript 126
Conclusion 130

CyberPunk Architects

On the go?

Get the audio version of this book for FREE when you sign up for a free Audible trial!

CLICK/TAP HERE

For UK Version GO HERE

Introduction

Congratulations on downloading *Hacking and Programming* and thank you for doing so.

This guidebook takes some time to look at the basics that you need to know about hacking, and how to get started with the programming language of your choice. The world of technology is changing and those who know how to handle it and who have the most knowledge about it are the ones who will get ahead. If you are a beginner who is interested in learning more and getting ahead, then this guidebook is the one for you.

The first section of this book is going to discuss the basics of hacking. We will look at the difference between ethical and black hat hacking, how to keep yourself safe, how to crack a password, and more. If you are interested in learning about hacking and what to know how to protect your own personal computer network and more, then the first section is a good place to start.

The second section of this guidebook is going to delve more into hacking. This section is going to talk more about the most common hacking threats that are harassing businesses and individuals today, how to do some man in the middle attacks, and more. This is a more advanced section that will help you to build on some of the skills that you learned in the first part.

Finally, the third section of this guidebook is going to explore how to get started with some of the most common coding languages. If you have ever been interested in learning more about the different coding languages and would like a taste of each one so you can figure out which to explore more in depth, then this is the section for you. We will look at some common coding languages such as C++, C#< C, JavaScript, and Python, all in one place!

There are plenty of books on this subject on the market, so thanks again for choosing this one! Every effort was made to ensure it is full of as much useful information as possible. Please enjoy!

Part 1
The Guide to Ethical Hacking for Beginners

Chapter 1: Setting Up a Hacking Environment

Before we start, it is important to realize that there is actually a ton of information out there on computers, which means that it can be impossible to learn all the things that you need to know in hacking. Many times people are going to specialize in just one field or area of hacking, such as networking, security of the computer, or software development. While you may not be thinking this far ahead as a beginning, but we are still going to look at some of the basic strategies that you can use when it comes to hacking. Later, you can take that knowledge and use it to fully understand the different possibilities that are open to you.

One essential thing that you need to do in order to get started is to know more about what is going on with the computer system. This is something that all hackers need to know. When you fully understand the system you are working with, it is easier to manipulate and modify the information that is there. If you go on a system and have no idea what is going on with it, it becomes hard to do any of the hacking work that we want to accomplish here.

Computer Programming

With hacking, knowledge is going to be your best friend. Moreover, the power that comes with hacking can be used both in good ways as well as in wrong ways. Of course, right now we are going to just focus on working with hacking in an ethical and moral way that will benefit yourself or the company you work for.

Some of the steps that you should consider using in order to get started with your hacking adventure include:

1. Take an interest in learning how to do various hacking techniques. You are reading this guidebook so we will assume that you are already to this point.
2. Know the basics of a programming language. It is hard to do well with hacking if you don't know anything about any of the coding languages. The programming language is important because it is designed to let you give your instructions to the computer. With this language, you are able to control how the computer behaves and even create or delete certain programs. If you don't already know a coding language, then it may be time to learn.

At this point, you may be curious about which coding languages you should learn how to use in order to get started with hacking. You can hack with pretty much any type of

13

coding language that you want, so if you already know one, go ahead and use that. If you don't know any hacking languages, then it is time to learn one. Some of the hacking languages that you may want to consider learning to help include:

Java: This is one of the most influential programming languages and it is easy to learn, works on many websites that you may need to hack, and it is free.
Python: This is a basic beginner's language that is free and open-source while still giving you a lot of power to get started.

Once you have chosen which programming language you want to work with, it is time to get that perfect environment set up. To do this, it is important to have certain devices on hand. Remember that you must be online and have a point-to-point protocol to make this work. If you do not have this thing, then you need to talk to your internet provider. The good news is that most DLS internet connections will have the PPP so you won't even need to worry about contacting your internet. Some of the other things that you may need to get started are some HTTP, network protocols, and network ports knowledge so you know how these things all work together.

The next thing that you need is an operating system that can work with the programming language you want to work on.

Computer Programming

Unix is often the most suitable system to work on for hackers. Unix operating system is a nice one because it is able to develop and then create software that will work on matter what system you want to try it on. Therefore, you would be able to create your own code and then use it on almost any other type of computer, something that is not always possible with some of the other operating systems. In addition, the Unix operating system is going to contain many utilities that can make hacking easier, such as a master program kernel.

We are going to assume that you are going to use the Unix system right now to make things a bit easier. This means that you must also get a shell account. This type of account is your user account that can give you access to the shell with the help of different protocols. These accounts are important because they can help with web space, software development, or file storage.

There may be times when you will want to use the Unix box as well. This is a computer that will run any of the operating systems that are under the Unix name, such as Linux. The Unix operating system and your Unix computer will be good for so many different things because they are able to tell you the difference in the servers very quickly. They are also good whether you need some security on the system, or you are using it for hacking purposes.

In order to get yourself started with this operating system, you have to choose between the free or the standard system. BSD or Linux are often the best, and most people will choose to go with Linux. This is because the Linux operating system is easy to use for most beginners. This operating system is also free so you will be able to do your work without having to spend a lot of money. Installing the system is pretty easy as well.

After you have the time to get all of this stuff, you will need to take some time to learn more about the Linux operating system so that you can use it properly. This is a pretty easy system to work with, but if you are used to working with the Mac OS or the Windows OS, then it takes some time to get used to it all.

Remember that the world of hacking is not always easy and you will need to work hard to be successful with it. You made the first step by showing an interest in the hacking, but now it is time to get started with more of the hacking and how you can use it for your own needs.

Chapter 2: How to Work with a Linux Terminal for Your Hacking Needs

As we talked about in the previous chapter, the Linux operating system is one of the best choices that you can use when you get started with your own hacking. This is because it is free and open-source so you won't every have to pay to use it and you can make changes to the code as needed without running into problems. The Linux operating system was originally designed to be used on personal computers, but because of how easy it is to use and all the versatility with it, it has been designed to work with many new platforms as well. In fact, it has been developed so much that it is now considered the most widely used operating system throughout the world.

Linux is considered one of the best, but we need to be able to understand how to work with the terminal properly, or you will never be able to hack with this system. To start with, we need to be able to distinguish what your terminal emulator is and why this is important. This terminal emulator is the program that will allow the usage of the terminal in a graphical environment. Today, it is common to see many people working with an operating system that has this graphical user interface already inside it, so it is something that you are already used to.

Another thing that you should be familiar with is the shell. The shell in the Linux operating system is the part that will read and then interpret the commands that you type into your code. It is able to read script files that you send to it and then tells your operating system what you want to happen. The neat thing is that there are many different shells that you can work with, including the Bourne shell or the C shell. Take some time to consider which shell you want to work with. While they have many similarities, there are some cool functions that are available in some and not in others.

Next, we need to move on to gain some knowledge about how the command prompt works. The message of the day will be the first thing that pops up any time that you log into the server. This message will contain any information that you need to know about the current version of Linux that is on your computer. After you have time to look at the message of the day, you will then be sent over to the shell prompt, which is often just known as the command prompt.

Inside this command prompt, you are able to send over tasks and directions to your server. The command prompt is where you are going to spend a lot of your time. You will need to write out the codes that you want to use or the directions that you want the computer to follow. All of this can be done from within the command prompt.

When you look at the shell prompt, you may notice that you are logged in under the name of "root". In this operating system, the root user is the one who is able to perform any administrative functions and tasks on the system. This is important that you have this kind of authorization on the system because it means that you can perform any kind of command that you want on the server because you are considered a superuser. Superusers will have unlimited powers when it comes to making commands, manipulating commands, and more on the server.

After looking through the shell prompt for a bit, it is time to look at the executing commands that are available as well. This occurs when you provide some commands to the server in your shell prompt. Therefore, you would take the time to specify the name of the files, listing them out as the script of a binary program. When working in Linux, there are many utilities that were installed before you even got it. These are nice to work with because they will allow you to navigate through the file system, configure the system how you want, and then install applications as you see fit. Giving commands to the shell prompt in this manner will be known as a process.

There are many different types of commands that you are able to provide inside of the command prompt. For example, with the right commands, you can use the command prompt to install your software package and do any navigation that you need through the system. When you use the command prompt to execute your commands in the front, you must make sure that the process has time to complete before you go to the shell prompt.

In addition, when doing commands, you must remember that the default is that everything is case-sensitive, including the options, the commands, the files, and the names of everything. If you are working on a command and find that it is not working the way that you think it should, the first thing that you need to look through is whether you did the right spelling on everything and if you used the right case on the commands.

You may also encounter some issues with the connection to the Linux server. Looking online can help you out best when you are looking for a solution to this problem.

Computer Programming

Writing out the commands is meant to be as simple as possible so that everyone is able to do it. To write out your command and get it to execute without any arguments, you would just type the name of the command that you want to use, and then press the return button. Commands that come like this, the ones that don't have any options or arguments, are going to behave in a different way compared to commands that have arguments. Of course, the behavior that you get for these will vary based on the command that you work on.

When we are talking about any of the commands that have an option or argument, accepting these can really change the way that the command is going to perform. Every argument is there to specify and direct the command in a certain way.

To make it easier to understand, the options are not going to be anything more than some special arguments that have been directed in a certain way. They are also important because they are able to affect and modify the behavior at the command prompt space. Just like with the arguments, options are going to follow the commands that you write and sometimes there are going to be over one option for the same command that you do. Options are distinguished as being single-character special arguments that often come with a descriptive character. However, both the options and the arguments are going to have more information about the commands that you are working on.

There are also a few variables that can show up in the environment that you work on. Environment variables are the ones that have the ability to change the behavior of the commands as well as the way that the command is executed. First, when you get onto your server, there are variables for your environment that are already set up based on how the file was configured. You will be able to run the "env" command in the command prompt to see all of the environment variables. The next step from here is to look for the path entry. This is the thing that will give you the directions about the shell looking for executable programs and scripts.

From this place, you will then be able to get the values of the variables with using the prefix of the names of your variable. Then add the $ character in front. When you do this, it automatically goes through and expands the variable to its value. If you do this and it comes up with an empty string, then you are asking the computer to access a variable that isn't set.

After you get some practice with the variables, it is time to learn how to set them. To set these variables, you simply need to type in what you would like to name the variable and then follow it up with the equal sign, and then the desired value. If you have a variable with an original value, this can be overwritten if you are setting the existing environment variable. If your variable doesn't exist, it will not after you use the above to set it. Command export makes it easier for you to export any variables that are inherited if you need.

When it comes to being able to reference or bring out any variables that already exist, you must make sure to add in the directory where it is located at the end of the command. This is also important when you add on or modify any of the variables because you must know where they are located on the computer, or your command prompt will get confused.

While the command prompt is up, take some time practicing your variables. You can name them anything that you want, just practice how you would go through this process, and look to see which directory they end up in so that you can pull them up later if you wish.

This was just a little introduction to the environment that you get to work with when you are on the Linux operating system. Make sure to play around with the environment and learn how all the different parts work. This will help you out when

CyberPunk Architects

we get to do some of our own hacking in the next few chapters.

Chapter 3: How to Make Sure That You are Anonymous Online

Being a hacker, whether you are a white hat or a black hat hacker, means that there will be some times when you will break into a system. Sometimes you will do it on your own computer to see how easy it would be for a hacker to get onto it, and sometimes you will get onto a system that you are not allowed to be on. Many times, you will be able to get into the system through the communication networks.

A hacker is able to use their knowledge and their ability with computer sciences for both illegal and legal activities. The first group is those who decide to get onto a network and modify things, steal personal information, and more. These types of hackers are considered criminals and can face steep charges if they ever get caught. On the other hand, there are also ethical hackers. These hackers sometimes get into a system that they have no authorization for, but they don't use the information in an unethical way. Ethical hackers are most likely individuals who work for a company and have the authorization to perform hacking activities in order to keep the company, and the information they have, safe.

In this guidebook, we are going to focus on just the moral and ethical hacking. Even though we are going to look at options that are more ethical and moral, keep in mind that the techniques that we talk about are going to be similar to what black hat hackers would do. This is because both hackers have the same process to get onto a computer system, but what they do when they get on the system can make the difference between whether they are white hat or black hat hackers.

As a hacker, it is your job to be able to get onto a network without being caught. If you get caught, then you will be kicked off. Even as an ethical hacker, you want to aim to get through the system without getting caught. Other hackers are going to try to do the same thing, and you are trying to find any loopholes in the system before some black hat hacker can beat you to it. To do your job successfully, you need to be able to remain anonymous while you go through the computer system and try to get on undetected.

If you look at a computer system, you may notice that there are a lot of restrictions and security measures that are put on in the hopes of keeping the computer as safe as possible. This is why it is only some of the best hackers who are able to get onto computer systems for big companies. Hackers must be able to stay anonymous with their work and not get traced by the tricks that are on the computer system, which can be tough when different measures are put into place, such as strong passwords and two-factor authentication.

At this point, you may feel that it is almost impossible to get onto a computer network that is not yours and remain anonymous. Some of the things that you can do to make sure that you aren't caught when doing your hacking will include:

1. First, make sure that you are not working with a Windows computer. While the Windows operating system can do many neat things, it is not the best when it comes to your hacking endeavors. Like we talked about before, the best operating system is one that is based on the Unix operating system, and most people choose to go with Linux.
2. When you try to hack, you want to make sure that any connection to the internet that you have is not direct. If you make a direct connection, then the other administrators on the network you are hacking will be able to trace you back through the IP address you leave. You should consider going with something like a VPN to help you share and receive files and data while you are online through a public network. You would be connected to your own computer while using the VPN just as you were using a private network. This can help

keep you secure and makes it a lot harder for others to find you.

What is a VPN and how will it keep me hidden?

A VPN is going to be your friend when it comes to remaining hidden while you work on connecting to a system that is not yours. It is a virtual private network and makes it harder for people to trace your IP address and find out you were on their network. This is a great way to keep you hidden and anonymous while you are doing some hacking.

To help you get connected to a VPN, you will need to make sure that you have some proxy servers that you can connect to. This helps to protect both your location and your identity at the same time. You used to be able to do this with a website online, but many websites are starting to block those who use the VPN technology in order to make sure that there isn't anyone entering unauthorized.

You do have another option with the VPN when it comes to hacking. This technology will allow you to create your own private tunnel. That way, when you are using this technology and someone tries to trace your IP address, all that they will see is the address that comes with your VPN. You get to have control over naming your VPN, so you can make it even harder to trace if you would like.

Which VPN is the best one to use?

You will quickly find that there are actually quite a few options for you to go with on your VPN. Some of the ones that are the best to ensure private browsing and secure browsing include PureVPN, ExpressVPN, and NordVPN. All of these options are free for you to use and download. Always do your research before downloading a VPN because some will have better features, better security, and work better than the others will.

When you are setting up your VPN or doing anything else with hacking, make sure that you never use your own email address. If you use your real email address, it could get connected with the VPN, and someone can trace it back to you. Instead of going with one of your own email addresses, you should go through an email service that is anonymous. These services allow you to get and send out emails without being traceable, especially if you use the VPN. When you go online, you can share this information if you would like, allowing you to still access the sites that you want, but making it hard for others to be able to find out who you are.

Which email software is the best to remain hidden?

Your email address is very important when it comes to hacking. You must make sure that it is anonymous and that no one will be able to trace it to help keep yourself hidden during this time. To make sure that your email address is meeting these criteria, you may want to consider downloading Hushmail's. This software is easy to use and doesn't come with a lot of advertising. There is a free version that has about 25 MB for storage, but if you want more than that, you will have to pay extra. You can also choose to go with another option that is known as Guerilla Mail. This is a nice option because the messages that you get in this email server are temporary and will disappear after an hour.

There are some email servers that aren't good to use with hacking because they don't offer the security and anonymity that you need with hacking. Google is not a good one to choose because it will store your IP address as well as all your cookies and searches. If you do decide to go with this email, you should find some services that will stop Google from remembering the online history you have. Some of the services that will do this include DuckDuckGo and StartPage.

Another thing that you need to consider is the type of wireless connection you are using. A public one may be convenient, but it is a big issue when it comes to the security of your hacking experiment. The problem is that each computer, including yours, has a unique address that goes with it. The router that is present in a public area is going to record the address.

When the public router tracks your IP address, this means that someone will be able to lead right back to the device and the location where you did the hack. Another problem that can come up with using a public Wi-Fi is common hacking attacks. Attacking on a public router is a man in the middle attack, and it is really going to compromise how hidden you are able to stay in your hacking attack and other endeavors.

With the man in the middle, attacks that you need to worry about are other hackers who will connect to the same network as you. They will then be able to get your information and then track you down. This can kind of ruin all the work that you are trying to do, and will mean that you are not able to complete your hacking attempt. It is best to not even try to do any hacking with a public connection.

These are just some of the basic tips and things to consider when you are trying to remain anonymous and keep your identity hidden while going online. These are tips that you can follow whether you are trying to stay safe online or if you are trying to hack.

CyberPunk Architects

Chapter 4: Setting Up NMAP

Now that we have taken some time to learn about the Linux terminal and how it works, as well as some of the precautions and tips that you can take to ensure that you are hidden and your identity is safe when hacking, it is time to learn how to set up your own NMAP. This stands for network mapper. The network mapper is a security scanner that you as a hacker can use to help discover hosts and services that are on a device.

The network that you look through for a computer is going to be filled with a lot of hosts and services that are anonymous. The NMAP is able to help you to track and discover these things and then it will put them together so that you can get your own personal map of the network. The way that this network mapper is able to do this is to send out special packets to different hosts, which will be the targets for this hacking project, and then the NMAP you have in place will be able to analyze the responses that it receives from these targets.

The network mapping software provides the hacker with a lot of great tools that you are sure to love. These can include detection of vulnerabilities on the network, operating system detection, and even discover of the host. These are the features that you will need in order to probe a network you are one. But these are just some of the basic features that you can choose. This tool is always being developed and changed so there are a lot of other cool tools that are coming out to make the NMAP more efficient.

As you can guess, there are a lot of times when this network mapper will be a good tool for you when hacking. It would be almost impossible for you to figure out the services and hosts that come with a network without the NMAP to help you discover them all. You would be able to use quite a few of these features, such as port scanning, scriptable interactions with your host, and determining the operating system that is on the network. You would be able to use this in order to help you generate traffic to your target, auditing how secure your server is at the time, and even finding out if there are any vulnerabilities that you or someone else would be able to exploit.

Now that we know a little bit more about the benefits of working with this network mapping, it is time to see how you would set up this kind of scanning for your own use. This may sound a little bit advanced, but it is actually easy to do and with just one command, you could get the NMAP installed on your computer. Let's look at how to get this done.

The first step that you need to do is check whether or not the computer you want to work with already has this network mapper installed. There are many platforms that will have this tool put on them already and if you are working with BSD or Linux, then you don't have to worry about installing this tool at all.

In order to figure out whether the NMAP is already on your computer, you just need to open up your terminal window. When that is set up, you can get it to execute the NMAP command. If the computer already has this tool on it, you will see that show up on your output. If the computer doesn't have this tool on it, and you put in that command, then it will come up with an error message. Even if you have the NMAP tool, it is a good idea to do an upgrade to make sure that you have the newest version.

NMAP is going to run off a shell prompt. This is nice because it lets you execute your commands without having to go through a lot of option fields and configuration scrips in the process. The NMAP tool is going to have many options that you are able to use in the command line, even some that you may not have to use that often. Interpreting and executing any type of outcome that you want is going to be easy once you learn how to make this command line function, and once you know which command line options you should pick.

Before we go on with that, you may need to install the NMAP. If you did the commands from above and found that your computer didn't have this tool installed on it, then now is the time to do it. You can get this from the website Nmap.org. You will be able to get both the binaries and codes from this. Your codes are going to be compressed files for you to use and the binaries will come in the platform that you choose, such as Windows or Linux.

After the binaries and the source codes are downloaded onto your computer, you will want to make sure that the integrity of the files and your maps are good. There are some packages that you can use to download the maps, but you always have to be careful that they aren't infected with a virus or a Trojan.

Therefore, when you are going through and verifying the files that you get, it is good to consult with the PGP signatures to see if they match up with the NMAP version that is on your computer. When you are downloading the NMAP, you are going to get the cryptographic hashes and the PGP signatures at the same time. You would just need to look in the signature directory to find these.

These are supposed to match up together, or you can look to see if it was signed with a special key. You can get the special key through the command line, and you only need to do this once. It helps you to verify the NMAP that you downloaded and makes sure that it is safe and legitimate for your computer. It won't do you any good to spend time hacking if the files you are downloading are infected and someone will be able to use those as a means to hack into your own computer.

Another option is to look at SHA1 and MD5 hashes to help you to do a validation on your NMAP. These are not as safe as the other options because these hashes come from third parties in most cases and it is possible that they could be corrupted or infected.

Once you are done verifying the NMAP through one of the means above, you can then use it in order to check out the hosts and the servers of a network from the source code that you provide to it. This is a great place to start because it gives you some insight into who is on a network, who may be the most vulnerable, and so much more.

Chapter 5: What are the Best Password Cracking Tools?

The next thing that we are going to look at is how to work with password cracking. If a hacker is able to crack a password, they are able to gain a lot of information on a computer. They could get onto the main system for a big company; they could gain financial information, and so much more.

There are several different ways that a hacker would be able to get ahold of a password on a computer. Some of the most common ways that they could crack these passwords include:

- Using a brute force attack. This can work, but it takes a lot of time since the hacker needs to go through every possible combination and hope that one works and that the user won't change their password in the process.
- Using a dictionary attack to help crack any passwords that are encrypted.
- With the hashes in order to crack any Windows passwords.

Computer Programming

- By looking at the wireless packages that they receive and then cracking either the WPA or the WEP passwords
- By looking in and recognizing the different injections and scripts that will discover hidden resources and scripts.

Let's look at some of the most common types of password cracking tools that you can use.

Aircrack-ng

This is a powerful tool that you can use to crack passwords. It is going to use a variety of features inside, such as WPA crackers, detectors, and analysis tools, to help you get the job. You can even find some tools to help crack passwords on a wireless LAN. It is going to work with the wireless network interface, which can handle a lot of traffic and can really help you to get ahold of the passwords that you want. It is also free for you to download and use and can work on the Linux operating system. It mostly will focus on being able to monitor and then capture packets from the target computer and then exporting the files so that third-party tools can look through them.

Crowbar

Crowbar is another option that you can use when trying to crack a password. If you want to do a brute force attack, then this is the one that you will choose to go with. When using this tool, you get a chance to be in control of what is submitted over to the web servers. Crowbar is not going to find the positive responses, but it will compare content from your responses on a baseline that you set. It is also free to work with, and it only works on the Linux system.

John the Ripper

When it comes to password cracking, John the Ripper is going to be the most popular. It is very effective and really powerful for this purpose. Cracking passwords will often mean recovering data from a lot of data that has been stored on your target network or computer. John the Ripper can help you to use a brute force attack as efficiently as possible. It can be downloaded for free, and for most hackers, this is enough, but there is a paid version if you would like something a bit more. It is able to work with many different operating systems and is one of the best in the industry for cracking passwords.

Medusa

Another great hacking tool that you can work with is the Medusa tool. This is another brute force password option that will provide you with some excellence when it comes to performance. One of the benefits of using this tool is that it allows you to use a thread based testing so that you can fight off more than one user or host at a time. Medusa was developed with some great features, such as allowing some flexibility in user input, and it is free to download. This one works on the Mac OS X and Linux and it can perform your attacks with a lot of speed, even against protocols like database, telnet, and HTTP.

Having a good password-cracking tool can make a big difference when it comes to how well you can hack. If a hacker is able to get ahold of the passwords for a computer or a system, then they are able to gain access to whatever else they would like. The tools and programs above will make this possible.

Chapter 6: What is the DarkNet?

As you get into the world of hacking, you may run into something that is known as the DarkNet. DarkNets are small parts of the Deep web, which is just a catch-all term for all of the net connected stuff that isn't as easy to find for some of the big search engines. Most of the stuff that show up in the Deep web end up there because they are cast offs. These would be some odd file formats or other queries from a database that these major search engines may not be able to handle or understand. This doesn't mean that anything is wrong with them or there is hidden information, just that they aren't formatted or used in the proper manner.

In comparison to the Deep web, the Darknet is going to be stuff that is deliberately hidden from any prying eyes when they search online. These files and website are going to use some specialized software to hide themselves so that they can remain anonymous and encrypted between the users. There are also some domains and protocols that most people on the web wouldn't even accidentally stumble across the sites when they did a search.

What this means is that the chances of being able to find these networks, much less the content that is hidden in them, is hard to do. Someone is going to have to point you over in the right direction before you even stand a chance.

Because of the difficulty that comes with finding things that are on the DarkNet and some of the illegal activities that have occurred because of the anonymity that comes with these websites, the DarkNet has received a bad name. However, there are some good things that could happen with this. For example, DarkNets would allow free speech, especially in countries that don't protect this kind of speech. For example, the Strongbox that comes from the New Yorker is a Tor Hidden service that allows whistleblowers to communicate their information to the magazine anonymously and securely, and this is just one example of how the DarkNet can be used in an ethical manner.

When you are going through the DarkNet, you will find that the publishers and searchers are going to always be anonymous. This happens because of the TOR software that is behind the service. Basically, when you work with a regular internet network, your computer will access the host server of whatever site you decide to visit. However, with the TOR software that is present on the DarkNet, you will have that link broken. The communication that you do will be registered, but TOR will prevent anyone from knowing who is behind that communication. This gives you complete freedom online and it can run on most of the operating systems out there.

While you may not want to spend your time looking through the DarkNet and spending time there, you can definitely use the TOR software and technology that comes with it to help keep your privacy and security in place. This software will ensure that you are able to keep your online activities safe from others. Everything that you do online on the regular internet will show up because websites like to hold onto this information. But the TOR software is a great one to consider because it lets you do your searching without anyone else being able to see what is going on and use that information against you.

Chapter 7: How to do Wireless Hacking

While getting the password of your target computer is a great way to get started with hacking, there are other things that you can do as well. Here, we are going to look at how to get started with cracking a wireless network. When you do this, you are attacking and then effectively defeating the devices that are supposed to keep a network secure. WLANs are wireless local area networks that are commonly known as Wi-Fi. WLANs may be popular, but they have a lot of security holes that make then vulnerable. Wireless security often comes up because of two factors: a weak encryption and a weak configuration.

While we are going to show you some of the steps that come up with wireless hacking, keep in mind that doing this kind of hack can be difficult to accomplish. Hackers will often have to try many times to make it happen and will have to rely on a number of strategies and techniques to see it work. If you keep on trying though, you may be able to see what holes there are in your wireless network and try to close it up before a hacker can get there. As a hacker, you are going to really need to rely on your physical skills, social engineering, and computer science knowledge to make this wireless network hack work.

If you are able to hack into a wireless network, you will be able to gain access to everything that you want from that network. The process is hard, but many hackers will decide that it is worth their time to do it because of all the information they can get after they are done.

You will quickly notice that there are many different options when it comes to wireless hacking. Some of the most common ones that you may want to consider include:

- Aircrack: This is one of the most powerful and one of the most popular tools that you can use when it comes to wireless hacking. This tool was developed so that it could use the best algorithms to help recover passwords simply by finding and then tracking down the relevant packets. Once it has captured the packet, Aircrack is going to use that information to find the password. In order to get the attack done at a faster speed, it is going to implement a standard FMS attack with better optimization.
- Airsnort: This is another tool that you can use any time that you want to be able to decrypt a WEP wireless network encryption. It is free to download on your

Computer Programming

computer and it can work on both the Windows and the Linux operating system. The way that this tool works is that it is going to monitor the keys and transmissions of the other computer in order to make up some packets to send back to the hosts. Due to how simple it is to use this tool, it is the perfect one for a beginner to get started on.

- Kismet: This one is known more as a network sniffer. Kismet is going to work with any type of wireless card that you decide to go with and it supports the rfmon mode as well. Kismet will work because it is able to collect and then receive the packets that you need in a passive manner and then it can help you to find any networks that are hidden there. This is a great one to use if you plan to work with the BSD, Linux, or OSX operating systems.

- NetStumbler: The next option that you can choose from on our list is the NetStumbler. Many people throughout the world use this hacking tool for all of their wireless hacking. It is one that will only work with the Windows system, but it is still free to use so it may be worth your time if you use that operating system. There is also a mini version that you can work with. This tool is used for a process called wardriving and it can also discover some access points that are unauthorized. The biggest issue with this tool is that it won't work well with the 64-bit Windows system. Nevertheless, it can help you collect a bunch of useful information off the network of your choice.

- inSSIDer: This is another great scanner that you can use when you are working with the operating system for Windows. This was a free tool in the beginning, but now it comes with a premium so if you want to use it, you may have to pay a little bit. There is a large variety of tasks that you can get this tool to do, but it also helps you to open up any access points that are wireless and it saves any logs that come in from the GPs.

- WireShark: This is another tool that you can use if you need a network analyzer. With this tool, you can put it on your own computer so you can get a good idea of what exactly is going on in your own personal network. You can easily do a live capture and then analyze the packets that are being sent through. You can use several modes to make it easy to look at a large amount of data fast or do it in micro-mode. It works on almost all of the operating systems so this is one of the best to go with if you want to make sure that it works on a variety of computers with different systems. Before you decide to go with this option, you need to make sure that you have some familiarity with network protocols.

- coWPAtty: Sometimes you may decide that it is a good idea to work with what is known as an automated dictionary attack. You can do this with the help of a Linux operating system. The command line is going to contain a word list with all the passwords that you may need to do the attack. This is good for those who are just getting started with hacking, but it is somewhat slow. It is going to use a dictionary to crack a password, which is a slow process that may not be that effective.
- Airjack: This is another wireless cracking tool that has many different people throughout the world to use it. Airjack is going to be an injection tool for a packet. What this one does is inject packets into a network and because there are so many packets that go through, the network ends up going down.

You may find that you are able to use a few different options from this list, plus more, in order to hack into a network. These networks do have some security protocols in place in order to keep people out of them. However, there is always a vulnerability that comes with these wireless networks, whether that vulnerability is from the network or from someone who is using the network. Moreover, by using a variety of these tools, you may be able to find that vulnerability and get onto the network of your choice.

Chapter 8: Basic Steps to Keep Yourself Safe from Other Hackers

When you get started with hacking, you will quickly find that there are a lot of different strategies and techniques that you can work with. However, you will also learn that there are many potential issues and hole in your own system, and you may want to go through and learn how to keep your own computer safe. With everything going online and becoming more digital than ever before, it is more important than ever to make sure that no one else is able to get on your own network or your own computer. Some of the ways that you can ensure that you keep yourself safe from others who may want to get your personal and financial information include:

Always take caution about what is shared online

With social media and our online world, it is easy to get caught up with sharing everything online. Be especially careful with some of those question-like posts on Facebook and other sites. They may ask your name, where you were born, your kid's names, where you went to school, and more. These may seem like some harmless fun, but they actually provide many hackers with valuable information that they can use to get onto your accounts. Only share a few things online and make sure to keep it protected with a very strong password.

Setting passwords that are strong and unique

It isn't a good idea to put in "password" or something similar in order to protect your accounts. A strong password, including one that is unique and hard to guess, will ensure that you are protected. You can take this even further by doing two-factor authentication. When you enable this two-factor authentication, you will need more than just your password in order to get onto an account. You may have to answer some security questions, get a unique code sent to you, or something else to verify you are supposed to be there.

Download the Password Manager Tool

Before you do any more stuff online, you may want to work with what is known as a password manager tool. This tool is able to save all of the passwords that you have to keep them safe. You can use any type that you would like but 1Password and Dashlane.

How LittleSnitch can help

Another option that you can consider working with is called LittleSnitch. Remember that we talked about how important it was to work with your own virtual private network in order to make sure that hackers and other intruders weren't able to get onto your own personal network and move the internet traffic the way that they want. LittleSnitch can also be put onto your computer network to help you stay safe. This program is able to monitor any connection that goes out of your network. Therefore, if there is a time when a computer is trying to send files over to an unknown server, it is going to alert you about this so that you know someone else is on the network. In addition, your laptop needs to be set up so that it works with full disk encryption. If you don't already, now is the time to turn it on.

Remember that you need a good antivirus program.

A good antivirus program can make a big difference in how safe your information will stay when you use your computer. Yes, these are not foolproof and even having one on your computer isn't a guaranteed way to keep the hackers out. Nevertheless, it certainly makes the job harder to do. These antiviruses, as long as they are kept up to date, can help you to keep viruses off your computer and they can do a good job against any trojans that a hacker may try to install. Adding in some other simply security plugins, such as ad blockers, can be a good idea to protect your computer as well.

If you use Flash, then it is time to stop.

If your computer uses flash at all, then it is time to stop using it and uninstall if you can. Flash is one of the most insecure software programs out there. It has a ton of holes in it that make this the perfect door into your computer for a hacker. There are many other great programs out there that you can use and get the same results, without having to put your computer at risk.

Take the time to do a backup of all your files on a regular basis.

No matter what security you have on your computer, it is always a good idea to do a regular backup on your files. You should do this when you don't have any connections to the network to make sure that someone isn't able to get onto the files when you are doing this process.

There are times when, despite your best efforts, someone will be able to get onto your computer and use ransomware. This virus will often ask to get personal information or money before being removed, but then the virus often stays on the computer, even after you comply. If you have a lot of important information on the computer, then you are stuck and may want to pay and deal with it to get those files back

However, if you go through and do a backup on a regular basis, you won't want to worry about it. The ransomware, or whatever other virus gets on your computer, may still be there, but you will still have the files, whether they are personal or not, at your disposal.

You should always be on the lookout for any threats or danger that could show up for your computer. Hackers are always trying to get ahold of your personal information, especially if it is financially related, and use it for their own needs. Using the tips above and always being on the lookout can make a big difference in how safe your information stays.

Part 2
Advanced Hacking Techniques

Chapter 9: The Top Cyber Security Threats Today

In our modern connected world, there are many threats to us being secure online. Many hackers have found that if they are just able to get onto the computer of their victim, they will be able to take whatever information they wish. Often they are looking to either gain knowledge, if they are working on a big corporation, or they want money, either with the target paying them or gaining the targets login information for financial documents. It is important to always be on the lookout and do what you can to avoid these kinds of attacks. However, it always feels like the hackers are a step ahead when it comes to what they are able to do to get on your computer. Let's look at some of the most common cyber security threats out there and how you can avoid them with your own personal computer.

Ransomware

The first cybersecurity threat is known as ransomware. This is when the hacker places something on your computer that blocks you from it. You often get a screen telling you that you must pay in order to gain access to your computer. Some of these are a little more advanced and will let you move around the computer, but will encrypt all of the files on your computer so you are no longer able to open them without a key. And of course, you won't be able to get around either of these two options or around any other type of ransomware without paying some money.

The amount of money that has been paid out for ransomware is staggering. In 2015, about 3.8 million was spent to ransomware, but it was up to 638 million in 2016, and the beginning of 2017 saw that over $209 million was being spent. This is a ton of money—way more than what is being earned with other cyber threats.

It also posses a bit issue for major organizations, although many of these attacks are going to occur towards individuals. Hospitals have found that they need to be super vigilant about these attacks because of the sensitive material that they hold onto. While most security experts recommend that you should actually pay the amount that the hackers are asking for with this virus, it is tempting to just go ahead and do it. Most hackers will put in a request for an amount that is affordable, and many mistakenly think that will be the end of their worries with the ransomware, so they pay for it.

There are a few different methods that ransomware can get on the computer of the victim, but the most common is Locky. This one often shows up as a basic word document and it will ask the user to go through and enable certain macros. Once this has been completed, the file will do a downloader in the background of the computer. This installs the ransomware software and will scramble all the data on each and every drive of the computer. And then it will demand that you give it payment to make the issue go away. The payment is often in Bitcoin to keep the security and secrecy going.

The biggest problem with this option is that there really isn't much you can do once you have the program on your computer. There is no good solution to clean up the mess after the fact. The best thing is to make sure that your information is backed up on some exterior drives so if you do get hit with ransomware, you at least still have the documents and files that you need.

IoT Botnet traffic

This is another concern that many companies need to watch out for. It is believed that more than 8 million devices are connected to the internet each year. This provides a lot of leeways for hackers to work on the most dangerous threat in the internet, DDoS, or distributed denial of service.

Let's take a look at how this can affect us with an example that happened in 2016. An extensive attack of DDoS was directed towards the DNS provider Dyp. This attack was done with the help of the Mirai botnet. It was launched at the same time from an unknown amount of IoT devices, likely at a Dyp customer. As a result of this attack, the entire structure of interest services, most of which were secure, were taken down. Some of the names that were affected in the process included the PlayStation network, Twitter, and Github.

What this shows is that when one of these attacks happens, it seems that a lot of the service providers are not really equipped to handle this large of an attack. With the example above, there were reports that there were actually other IoT bots that were recruiting botnets before that attack occurred. However, this is one of the biggest threats that is going on around us for online work today, and it can quickly take over even some of the bigger companies and make it hard for them to even function. With this attack, those big names went completely offline and weren't able to work properly, giving the hacker plenty of time to get on and mess around.

Phishing and Whaling

Phishing attacks of all kinds have been a big threat for a very long time. However, since more internet users are becoming familiar with them, the hackers are becoming more targeted with their attacks. A phishing attack is going to be when a fake email is sent to you from a company that you would normally trust. The intention is to get you to click on the email or insert personal and private information so that the hacker on the other side can have it. This could include financial information to get onto your bank account, or asking you specifically to send money. Often the target thinks that they are giving their information to a reputable site, at least until they are done with the attack.

Whaling is another thing to watch out for. This is the same kind of process, but the attack is going to focus on targeting an individual who has a high net worth. Often, this individual is going to be within the organization where the email comes from. The goal here is to get that individual to send over money to a fraudulent account.

While most people think that they would be able to avoid these kinds of attacks, they are still happening all over the place. For example, Mattel's financial executive once managed to lose $3 million because he thought that he was doing a legitimate request with a bank in China known as the Chinese Bank of Wenzhou. This is a larger scale example of this kind of attack, but it can still happen to almost anyone.

Machine learning enabled attacks

Artificial intelligence has really grown by leaps and bounds recently. Organizations and other big companies have been using this kind of technology for years to help them to grow and get certain tasks done. While this technology is extremely useful for a lot of companies, it is also something that you need to be wary about when it comes to a hacking attack.

Any time that you are able to combine information that is available publicly with some complicated tools for analysis, along with some other capabilities that come with machine learning, then it is possible to become a target with a hacker. In fact, hackers can easily use this information and technology against a big company in order to create a highly targeted and successful hacking campaign against whomever they want.

In a report from Intel Security, machine learning tools are actually forcing different multipliers for those who are actively involved in a variety of security roles. Of course, as a business, you must assume that if you are using these powerful tools, then it is likely that a hacker is, or will be, using those same tools as well.

Machine learning has done some wonderful things for companies. It can go through complex data and find patterns more efficiently than people can. It is the technology behind search engines. And it can do so much more. But for everything that a legitimate and ethical business can do with it, a hacker can jump on and do the same things. And this can cause a lot of headaches for companies who are not prepared for this.

As you can see, the number of threats to your security when you are online are rising like crazy. For every new security feature that is put in place, hackers are often able to find some backdoors and other ways to get around them and get your information. This is why it is important for both individuals and companies to be aware of the different attacks that can happen and prepare as much as possible to avoid them. This can help keep information safe and will make the job harder on the hackers.

Chapter 10: Laying Down the Ground Rules for Hacking

Now that we know a little bit more about the biggest threats that are out right now, it is time to know some of the basics about hacking because this is really of interest to a lot of people. Remember that there are differences between ethical hacking and black hat, or illegal hacking. Ethical hacking is something that more and more people are starting to understand and are expressing a need for learning more about. Here, we are going to focus our efforts more on the ethical hacking, even though many of the techniques are the same for ethical and unethical hacking, and then lay down some of the advanced knowledge that you need to know to get started with hacking ethically.

What is ethical hacking?

This is actually a new term in the hacking world. It is going to describe someone, either a company or an individual, who will use the techniques reserved for hacking in order to identify any threats that are present in a network and then close them up. The ethical hacker will have the same goal as a black hat hacker; mainly, they want to be able to try to bypass the security on the system by searching for those weak points they could take advantage of. Once they are done with their search, a report is going to be written in order to show where the strengths and weaknesses in the system are.

The idea of the work of an ethical hacker is that they are supposed to find these weak spots before a hacker does. They can then use this information to help minimize or eliminate the risk that the network has of an attack.

What constitutes ethical hacking?

When working as an ethical hacking, everything that you do with the process needs to be deemed ethical. This means that the following needs to occur before you start:

- You need to have the permission of the organization that owns the network before you get started. This needs to be in writing in most cases. If you work in the IT or the security department of a company, then you already have this permission. In addition, the intentions that you have for hacking onto the network need to be solely to identify any risks and then help fix them.
- You need to respect the privacy of the company or the individual you are working with.
- When you are done with your work, you must make sure that you are able to close out of it without any

breaches or new issues that another hacker is able to exploit later on.
- You must write up a report and give it to the proper people to show where you found vulnerabilities in the system.

Even with all the good that an ethical hacker can do for big companies, these professionals can still receive some criticism for their work. No matter what type of hacking it is, the hacker is still trying to get onto a network and expose its vulnerabilities for a specific reason. A black hat hacker is doing it for their own benefit, usually for some financial gain, while an ethical hacker is doing it in order to protect themselves or to protect a company.

As an ethical hacker, you must remember to remain the best integrity possible while doing the job. Your whole job is to make sure that a system is protected and that other hackers are not able to get onto them. You also must have permission to be on the network as well. Even if you only have honorable intentions, the company you hack is not going to be happy to find that you got onto their system and they could take legal actions. Always get permission and follow the rules and privacy settings of a particular company, and you are good to go.

How do I actually protect myself?

Let's say that you run your own business. One of the main responsibilities that you have in this position is to make sure that the operations are able to run as efficiently as possible and that you've cut out risks as much as you can. This means that you want to make sure that your information is safe and that any private information that you hold onto for customers will remain safe and secure and away from those who shouldn't have access to it.

Despite this, it is true that many business owners, whether they own a small business or a big business, fail to keep up with this responsibility. A survey that was done in 2012 by Symantec found that about 83 percent of small businesses didn't have any kind of cybersecurity plan for their business. In addition, about 69 percent of companies reported that they didn't even have an informal plan for cybersecurity, even if they did conduct business online.

What this information shows is that these companies are either unaware of how dangerous the internet is, or that they don't think it is something that they need to worry about. They are wrong on both accounts and the consequences of ignoring this threat can be devastating.

The biggest reason that many companies ignore the threat of the internet is that it is easy to believe that data breaches, hackers, and lawsuits that occur because of the above are just a tiny percentage of things that happen online and that they are isolated incidents. However, these cyber attacks could end up costing a lot of money for a business.

No matter what size of business you are in, it is important that you always protect your business when you are online. This is true whether a similar attack has happened in your industry or not. This can help you keep the trust of your customers in place and will protect you as well.

What are some of the ways that I can stay protected from cyber-attacks?

The good news is that to help protect the different information that your business hold onto doesn't have to be difficult. In fact, many of these are things that you should already be doing whether we talk about your personal accounts or a business account. Yes, many of the attacks that are done by hackers seem pretty advanced and intelligent, but many reports state that the individuals who are targets often aren't putting the right effort into protecting their computer networks.

According to a study done by Verizon, about 80 percent of the targets of these cyber-attacks were ones who were targets of opportunity. This means that these individuals were targeted because they had poor to no security on their networks. Having some kind of security in place will make a big difference. It may not prevent all attacks, but it certainly is something that you should do to keep you safe. Some of the things that you can do to help keep your business network safe from attacks include:

- Keep an antivirus on the computer: Malware is one of the leading tools used in information breaches. This can be planted directly to the laptop or PC that is on your network, it can be found on emails, it can be found on websites, and even through what you thought was a secure connection through Wi-Fi. A reliable anti-virus software can go a long way to ensuring your system is safe.
- Make sure that you are encrypting information: Anything that you send that has sensitive information, such as information about your employees or bank account information, must be encrypted. This type of information is important to hackers and encrypting it ensures that no one is going to see it.
- Educate all the employees: Many times hacking attacks occur because of human error, and this could come

from your employees. Make sure that all employees pick strong passwords to use on all account, ensure that they don't share this information, and help them to use every precaution possible to keep your business computer network safe.
- Check on the hardware. You want to always check that any hardware that you have is stored in a safe manner. A CCTV or a locked room will often be enough to keep it safe.

Consider hiring an expert to help

This is so important. Your business needs to have someone, or even a department if the business is larger, who is responsible for the security of your network. They will be able to do checkups on the network, do a comprehensive penetrative testing, and more to make sure that a hacker isn't able to get onto your network and take your information.

It is so important to make sure that the security of your computer network is in place. You are holding onto a lot of personal and financial information for your clients, and it is likely that a hacker will take advantage of any holes in the system in order to get the information that you have.

Chapter 11: The Procedures for Proper Cybersecurity

The first thing that we need to look into is what cyber security is and why it is so important to learn about it. It is important to understand that we are in the middle of what is considered a technological revolution and that truth is that technology is really involved in how we conduct our every day lives. Technology is important no matter what part of the country you are in and it is the single most important thing that will determine whether a country is considered advanced or not.

Technology can drive your success, and it is going nowhere without the help of the Internet. Moreover, when you spend time online, there is a lot of trouble that can present itself. While the internet can be a great thing to access and transfer information to anyone in the world, it also opens up the possibility that someone can intercept the information, or find a way onto your network without being invited.

To help you better understand more about cybersecurity and why it is an important thing for many countries, let's look at an example. Imagine a sturdy safe that is full of all the money in your country. With the first glance, you may think that your money is secure, but it is possible for the safe to get breached. Someone can learn the password or even use some brute force to get into the safe. In addition, when that happens, all of your money is gone and it can be hard to get it back.

The same kind of idea can go on the internet. The information that you store on the computer has the potential to be sensitive and personal depending on what your business does. Moreover, if this information ends up getting into the wrong hands, it could be dangerous. The problem occurs when the information is accessible any time the computer connects to the Internet. Hackers are waiting for this to happen so that they can get ahold of any information that is sensitive but put on computers that don't have the right security. This is also why a lot of organizations and governments will spend a ton of money to make sure that they are protected from hackers and have the best cybersecurity.

It is so critical that you understand how important cybersecurity is and how much of a difference it makes to your business and the network that you are using. You don't want to let someone who doesn't have the right authority to access the information in your system. Information is key and your customers trust you to keep their personal and financial information as secure as possible. Whether you are holding onto medical records, credit card information, billing information, or something else, it is important to keep this information safe and secure and ensure that hackers and others don't get ahold of this information and use it for their own personal gains.

Because of how important cybersecurity is, it is important to learn what things you need to do in order to assess whether there is a threat to your network and then learn how you could try to prevent this threat from being successful. When it comes to your computer network, there are many different things that you need to look over and account for. In some cases, the entity that is doing the report may ask you to go through some certification to make sure that you can maintain the security that is needed to protect your system.

Let's look at some of the things that you will need to go through in order to assess which threats are heading your way and how you will be able to prevent them as much as possible.

Doing a vulnerability assessment

The first thing to work on is a vulnerability assessment. This is important because it helps you determine the extent and the depth of the cyber defenses that you already have. This happens when you evaluate these defenses when you put them up against some patterns that happen with a real-world attack. You may be surprised at how lacking your defenses are

Computer Programming

when you see how they behave in these attacks, but it is a great place to start to see how far you have to go.

The consultants who are doing this kind of assessment are going to utilize methodologies that allow them to end up with real-world scenarios to see how your defenses would work if a hacker actually tried to get onto the system. When they are done, they will also provide a report on the best recommendations that you can follow in order to prevent these attacks in the future.

Penetration testing

Penetration testing is another important step to take in this adventure. With Network Architecture being the backbone of every corporation nowadays, it is mandatory that its security is not overlooked and regularly maintained. New attack methods and vectors are being introduced daily, which might leave your organization vulnerable to the ever-changing world of hacking, and experts are more than welcome to help you tackle the challenge of securing your information. Companies can provide you with the insight you require in order to maintain a safe and satisfying work environment.

In order to provide a comprehensive Penetration Test, consultants utilize real-world exploitation techniques to find any security loopholes within your Cyber Security perimeter.

Experts utilize advanced tactics to determine whether your important assets are at risk and can be exfiltrated by a malicious individual, thus providing you with an exact understanding of the extent of damages your company could face.

Web application assessment

If you have a web application as part of your business, then you must make sure that you do an assessment of this web application. These websites are vulnerable to an attack by a hacker so checking all the vectors to make sure that they are fortified against malicious attacks can be critical. These types of assessments are able to identify the vulnerabilities that your company may not be taking care of and can give you some capabilities to fix these issues. This ensures that you are able to keep your website and your web presence going well online without being hacked.

Network architecture security assessment

Something that has become a regular part of most businesses is the Bring Your Own Device or BYOD. Yet, the security of this is something that is often overlooked. It is also a common feature to provide all employees, or quite a few of them, with mobile devices, but then these devices, even though they can hold important and sensitive information for the company, will fall into a kind of a gray area with IT security. This means that many times, the IT security won't provide the same security on them as they will other online features for the business. This can provide some easy access into the business for the hackers and opens the door to get into other parts as well. Make sure that you trust the experts or the IT team in your business to look through even the mobile phones that you give your employees, to make sure all your bases are covered to prevent any security breaches.

Mobile device and application assessment

There has been a big growth in the IT field and this is going to come straight to your business, no matter what kind of business you are running. However, there are some chances that your business focus has left some of your security systems without the right procedures, policies, and mechanisms in place. If you don't have your own IT department, this is something that can easily happen without you having any idea. In addition, it is also possible that the IT part of your business is handled well and does the work that it is supposed to, but then the business still has some procedures and policies that are hard to track and enforce.

Taking the time to look over and track your policies and various procedures can make sure that you understand the areas where your business is lacking so that you can fix that before any big issues occur. This helps to reduce the amount of IT risk that you have and can reduce the impact of any security breaches if they do occur.

Information security management

While there are a lot of organizations that are working with digital forensics, many of them do not have the right tools, such as administration, procedures, infrastructure, or other requirements, in order to make sure that this field is going to work properly. You must work with some forensic experts to help you go through all of this so that you can effectively investigate what is going on before a hacker gets in. It is important that you are ready to either optimize or build up your entire process, maintain a good forensic laboratory that is pristine, and fortify your capabilities to keep hackers out of your company.

Mobile device forensics

Almost everyone has a mobile device now, and this includes many of your employees. This is true whether or not you provide your employees with their own mobile device or they rely on one of their own to help them out. You need to be careful with the phones that are provided or used to handle anything for your business. These are often not going to contain the same kind of security that you will find on computers or other items that are on your network. Moreover, if your employees are careless with how they use the phones, then this could result in trouble. you must make sure that there is enough security on these mobile phones, that employees know the proper procedures to follow when it comes to their mobile phones, and ensure that as much security as possible is used to protect information that is shared on these mobile devices.

Network forensics

When we are talking about cybersecurity, the network forensics is going to be the process of acquiring, analyzing, and processing network events to help estimate the surrounding details of cyber incidents and security attacks. This helps you to get a good idea of how secure your network is and can compare your network to some of those who have already been under attack. This gives you a good starting point to go from when you are trying to enhance your own security.

Web and internet forensics

It is likely that you and some of your employees will spend some time online, especially if you have a website that helps you run your business. The web and internet investigation is going to look at any internet activity that goes on to provide you insight on whether that could be causing some issues with the security of your company.

Malware analysis and reverse engineering

These are going to take some time to look into gaining a better understanding of certain pieces of software. When you have this understanding, you are better able to understand how they behave and can even start to better recognize how a cyber attack could happen. This information is so important in helping you to recognize cyber threats and detect and prevent them from happening in the future. It can even provide you a good view of any security gaps that are present and a look at any gaps in the chain of events that would make it easier to introduce malware into your network or into the system.

Insider threat assessment

Sometimes the threat is going to come from your employees. This doesn't mean that they are out to harm you. However, if they don't set strong passwords or are likely to open an email that looks suspicious, this could result in a security breach. This kind of assessment is going to look at some of the potential risks that you could face from employees or other knowledgeable personnel.

Things to consider when it comes to mobile device security

In our ever-changing world, one of the biggest areas where you need to be careful with the security of the information your business protects is with mobile phones and devices. While many companies will work hard to make sure those tablets and computers are safe when they are connected to the internet and to the business network, they sometimes forget that there needs to be some added security when it comes to a mobile device.

Much of the business world has moved to their phones. Mobile devices are almost like computers in some cases, and when you are out and about getting stuff done, it is sometimes easier to send emails and do business on your phone. This often results in a lot of information being put on the mobile device, without a ton of security being there to help protect that information.

The reason that this is a big issue is that many businesses have a ton of their information in a mobile environment. Even as an individual, you may have your social media accounts, banking accounts, and more set up as apps on your mobile device. Without the right kind of security, a hacker could easily get on the phone and get ahold of your passwords and more before stealing your money and your information.

In the process, many things could be damaged. And this can be a devastation no matter who you are. As an individual, it can result in you having someone get passwords to your personal information, such as banking, social media, and more. You could even lose pictures, documents, and more and getting it back can be hard.

When it comes to a business, there could be even more devastation. If a hacker is able to get onto the right mobile device, they will be able to take all of your sensitive information and cause some irreparable issues to your business. This is why it is so important for you to learn how to secure your data, not only on the computers that are linked directly to the network but also on your mobile devices.

Failure to put some safeguards on these mobile devices, and failure to make sure your employees know the importance of keeping that information safe on any mobile device they conduct business on, can be so important. It can make the difference between keeping customer information safe and secure or having to deal with a big cyber-attack that could cost you millions of dollars and make it so that the customer loses trust in you.

As you can see here, there are many things that the ethical hacker is going to need to understand and learn how to handle to make sure that the network of a business is able to stay as safe as possible. This is one of the biggest reasons why you want to really stay on top of the cybersecurity that you have. This is not always an easy task to undertake, which is why some companies choose to just ignore it altogether and assume that the attack will never happen to them. However, these attacks can happen to anyone and once they happen to you, it can really cost your business in a multitude of ways. Make sure that you have a dedicated team or company to handle this security so that you don't have to deal with the after-effects of a cyber-attack and what it can mean for your business once it happens.

Chapter 12: Should I Change My IP? Things to Consider During Infrastructure Monitoring

The next topic that we are going to look at is the IP on your computer. The IP is going to tell others where your computer is and can open up many doors to what you have been doing and your internet browsing history. This is such valuable information for other hackers to use. Even if you are the hacker, you don't want that IP address giving away your location, or you could end up getting caught in your work.

Changing your IP address is a great way to mask your digital footprint. It makes it so that crawlers have a hard time detecting your information and targeting you as a prospective lead. This makes it easier to get rid of geo-targeting and content-targeted ads just to name a few. The good news is that changing the IP that you use on your computer isn't that complicated. Let's look at how to change your IP address.

Regardless of the type of operating system you are using, whether it is a Linux, Mac, or Windows operating system, you will find that changing the IP of your computer is handy many times. If you have trouble logging onto some websites using a Chrome Browser, or on your smartphone, this could simply be because the IP that you are using isn't accepted.

In addition, there are times when you want to make sure your IP is hidden for your own personal reasons. You may not want to allow others to figure out who you are online or you want to make sure that your personal information is as safe as possible. Let's look at how you would be able to do this exactly.

Every time that you decide to connect your computer to the internet, the internet provider that you use is going to assign an IP address to that computer. This IP address is important because it allows the websites and other applications that you visit to keep track of what you do online. In some cases, these can even pinpoint your physical location based on this IP address. To help prevent the websites from being able to do this, you will need to go through and change your IP address.

The best way to get that IP address changed is to use a VPN proxy. This is a secure method that is also really fast to work with. There are many VPN service provides that you can choose. Some of them are offered free, and some are not. It will just depend on your own personal preferences. However, no matter which one you choose to go with, they are going to help you out in several ways. You will be able to bypass the regional blocks that are in place so that you can access any site that you want. This can be helpful if you don't want a program knowing where you are, either to keep your privacy or if you want to get onto sites that are restricted to just certain areas.

You can also choose to change your IP simply by restarting the router. You need to know ahead of time whether your ISP gets dynamic IP or not. If your ISP does get this, then the only thing you will need to do is turn off the router for a few seconds, no longer than a minute, and then turn it back on. This simple process will be enough to assign a new IP to your computer.

Keep in mind that this is a helpful thing to do if you are planning on spending some time with online gaming. There are plenty of games that will restrict its users based on their physical location and the only way that you are able to get through this restriction is to change your IP address. You will then know that your IP is going to be untraceable at that time unless it goes through a severe process, and even then, it is not guaranteed that someone will find out where you are from. And if they do, you can just go through the process again and change that IP address.

Changing your IP address on a regular basis can make a big difference in your business. It will help you to be able to get onto systems that you want, to stay safe online because people can't track you as easily, and so more. This should be one of the basic tools that you use as a hacker when you first get started to make sure that you are not easily traced.

Of course, there are going to be a number of other considerations that need to be accounted for. This is even truer when you are running a business. Sure, going through and changing your IP on a regular basis can be a great way to help you to stay safe, but it's not always the most effective method if you are a business. There are a few other things that you need to take into consideration including:

- Endpoint security: With the help of endpoint security, something that is a fundamental concept of a good and efficient organization's structures, companies are able to make sure that you are prepared to deploy it. Experts are going to have a solid knowledge of the bleeding edge solutions that can fortify your infrastructure.
- Network security: The IP address change is not going to do you any good if you are not able to keep your network security up and working well. You need to make sure that your network is up to date and that you

have all the industry standard implementations in place to keep your business safe from outside attacks.

- Infrastructure monitoring: You need to look at the depths of your IT infrastructure and check to see how your business processes are going to affect your security. The solutions that come with this would be able to help with your online presence, servers, and applications.

Changing your IP address is a good start to protecting your information online but it is just one of the first levels of security. If you are an individual, you may be able to get away with doing this and staying safe. Nevertheless, this should not be your whole plan when you are a business who is trying to protect sensitive information for your customers.

Chapter 13: Methods and Techniques for Hacking Like a Professional

Now that we have spent some time learning about how to avoid being a victim of a hacking attack and how you can start to become a professional in the hacking world on your own, it is time to do some of the techniques that are common in hacking. This is something that you need to know as an ethical hacker to help you get started with testing a network and making sure that it is as safe as possible. If you don't know how some of these techniques work, then it is impossible for you to do your job properly. Let's look at some of the techniques that you can use in order to hack onto a network

How to hack administrative passwords

The first thing that we are going to learn how to do is hack an administrator password on a Windows computer. Even on Windows 10, this is still something that hackers are able to do if the target doesn't use a strong password. The first thing to understand is that there are actually a number of tools that you can find online that will make it easier for you to attack different accounts, including mobile devices, WhatsApp, Viber, Facebook, Skype and more. However, when you are trying to hack into an administrator account password on Windows 10, there are a few things that you need to do, and they won't require you getting the external software to help.

Before you are able to do anything on an account, such as resetting the passwords on any of the non-administrator accounts, you need to be the administrator and have all the privileges that come with that. The steps that you need to follow to make this happen include:

1. Open up your command prompt on the Linux operating system. You would be able to do this by hitting Start, Run and then type in "cod" before pressing on Enter.
2. After you get to this point, you can type the command "net user" and then hit Enter again.
3. The system will then list out all of the user accounts on the system and on the computer. To keep with this example, we are going to work with the account that is named Patrick.
4. From here, you would go to the command line and type in "net user Patrick" and press Enter. Now the

system will ask that you enter in a new password for this account. If you did this successfully, you are able to change the password on the Patrick account without him having any idea.

This is a fast and easy way for you to go through and hack into every Windows 10 administrator password, as long as you have the right privileges in place to do so. This is a nice trick to know in order to restrict access to a computer. For instance, parents could put some parental controls on the computer they give to their teenagers. However, if the teenagers are able to get onto the administrator panel, then they would be able to overrun these restrictions and the parents would have no idea. It is a quick and easy method to work with, but there are other methods to use that are better sometimes.

How to hack a WhatsApp account

WhatsApp is one of the most commonly used messenger systems that people love to use. This is why learning how to hack into an account with this system could be really helpful sometimes. The easiest ways to do this is to get some designated software that is able to spy on a particular user and capture all of the personal information, including the password and the account name. These programs can be efficient, but they are going to cost you some money and you have to make sure that you are getting one that is good and that is able to get the job done for you.

You can use this kind of idea on many different accounts. You can spoof the address of any computer and gain access to bank accounts, to Facebook accounts, and so much more. Hackers are constantly working to do just this, which is why it is always important to set up strong passwords to keep information as secure as possible.

MAC Address spoofing: Doing it the hard way

Of course, you could go through and do address spoofing on a computer with some software, but you can also spoof it as a target smartphone through your own phone. This method does prove to be a bit more complicated and it can time you a bit of time before you see success. It is not necessarily hard, but it does require a few more steps from you to get it done, along with a few technical skills some of the steps that you can take to make this happen include:

1. Find the MAC Address of the phone that you would like to target. To do this, you first need to figure out if you are working with an iOS or Android phone.
   a. If it is an Android phone, you can go to Settings, then About Device, then Status, and then click on Wi-Fi Mac address.

b. If it is an iOS, you can go to Settings, and then General and About, and then click on Wi-Fi address.
2. Once you have the address for your target phone, it is time to spoof it.
3. When you do this, you will be able to get the address that you want. You can then install WhatsApp on your own phone and use the phone number from your target. This results in you having an exact replica of that account and all the messages will come to you.

Even though this method does take some time and some technical skills to do, it is not that complicated to get the information for the WhatsApp account. This means that many other hackers may try to do the same thing. Being careful with these services is important to ensure that someone is not able to get onto your account and do what they want with it.

Part 3
The More You Know: Learning How to Code with Several of the Best Programming Languages

Chapter 14: How to Code with C#

There are so many different coding languages that you can choose to work with. Some are better for working on website codes, some are better for beginners, and others that are really powerful and can work well with security and some of the other powerful programs you will want to create. To get us started though, we are going to look at some of the basics of coding with the C# programming language.

C# is a very popular coding language, but it is a bit tougher than some of the others that we will learn in this section. For how much power comes behind this coding language, you will like that it is actually easy to learn. Before you get started with some of the information and the codes that we are going to discuss, make sure to download the C# language onto your computer by visiting the following website: http://www.microsoft.com/en-us/download/details.aspx?id=7029

Getting started with the variables

Variables are the first topic we are going to discuss when it comes to the C# is the variables. These variables are the names that you will give to your data inside the program you write. These data types are ones that you will want to store for now but then manipulate later on as you work on the code. For example, if you would like to be able to store the age of the user in the program, you would be able to name that with the variable userAge, and then declare it with the following statement:

int userAge:

This statement will declare the state of the type of data you are using and the variable it goes with. It also lists out the name of that data type so that you are able to refer to it later on. Depending on the type of code that you are writing, you may have some text or some numbers that would name the variable.

Since this exampled relied on the variable named (int), the code will show that there is an integer inside, which is perfect for this example since we want to get an age. The program, after you are done labeling that variable, is going to save a bit of space in the computer's memory to store this data. This makes it easier for you to come back and find the variable and access any data that you want, just by bringing up that same name later.

What data types will I use in C#

The next question that you may have is what data types are going to be important with the C# coding language. There are several types of data that you are able to work with. Some of these are important so we are going to look at them before moving on. These include:

- Int: This data type is for integer. This is some kind of number. In fact, it can be any kind of number as long as you don't include a fraction or a decimal inside of it.
- Char: This is for character. This is any unit that comes in your code. You can write out a code that has one character, or you can add together many characters to come up with a more complete code in the end.
- Bool: This is for Boolean and any time you use this in our code, it is going to rely on true and false. This can help with some of your control flow statements because it checks to find out if the answer is true or false simply by going off the conditions that you set.
- String: This data type is going to be used when you would like to compare, manipulate, and create some text that is found in your code.

The operator is another popular data type that is used in the C# language, especially if you are just getting started out. These operators can do many different things in you're the operators can work by assigning a value to your variable, they can add some variables together, and so much more. There are actually a few different types of operators, but the ones that you are most likely to use in your coding with C# include:

Arithmetic operators

These operators are the ones that allow you to do various types of math in your code. If you would like to add or subtract a few of your variables at a time, then you would need to work with the arithmetic operators for example. Some of the most common operators that fall into this category include:

- (+): this is the addition operator.
- (-): this is the subtraction operator
- (*): this is the multiplication operator
- (/): this is the operator for division
- (%); this is the modulo operator
- (++): this is the increment operator and is used to increase the value of your operand by one.
- (--): this is the decrement operator and it is used in order to decrease your operands value by one.

Relational operators

Computer Programming

The arithmetic operators are probably some of the most common ones you will rely on in your code. However, there are also times when you will need to work with the relational operators. These operators are able to take two operands in your code and decide whether they are not equal or if they are equal. These operators will then give you the proper results at the end. Some of the relational operations that you may need to work with include:

- (==): This operator is the equal one. If you have two values or operands that are equal, then you get a result that is true.
- (!=): This operator will be the one that tells you the two values are not equal.
- (>): This operator will tell you if one value is greater than the other.
- (<): This operator is going to tell you if one value is less than the other.
- (<=): This operator will tell you if a value is less than or equal to the other.
- (>=): This operator is going to tell you if one value is greater than or equal to the other.

When you add a relational operator to your code, remember that these are going to be Boolean data types. What this means for your program is that the answer you get from them will be either false or true. If you get a return of true from your code, this means that the statement is connected to your code and it will execute. But if the statement or the return is false, the code will end. If you worked with a conditional statement here, then the second statement will be the one that shows up on the screen if you get a false response here.

Logical operators

Next on the list to know are the logical operators. These are ones that can help you do a few cool things inside of the code, and some of the most common ones that may show up in the C# code include:

- (&&): This operator is known as the AND. It shows up in the code if both of the operands you are working with are true.
- (||): This is the operator that is known as OR. This will give you a true answer if at least one if not both of your operands are considered true.
- (^): This operator is the exclusive OR. It is going to show up if one of the operators in your code is true.
- (!): This operator is able to change, or reverse, the value of a Boolean variable.

The logical operators are often seen as similar to the relational ones because they rely on Boolean answers as well. Your return with this logical operators will either end up being false or true based on the conditions that you add to the code and the answers that the user gives to you.

Working on a code

While these are just a few of the basics that you need to begin writing a code in the C# language, we are going to take our discovery to the next step and write out some of our own codes. Make sure to open up your C# compiler and then type in the following code to get us started:

using System;
using System.Collections.Generic;
using SystemLinq;
using System.Text;
using System.Threading.Tasks;

namespace HelloWorld
{

    //A simple program to display the words Hello World

    class Program
    {

static void Main(string[] args)
{
   Console.WriteLine("Hello World!");
   Console.Read();
}
}
}

As you try to type this into your compiler, you may notice that on occasion, there will be a little box that shows up on the screen that is giving you some help or some tips. This is the Intellisense part of the program and it is helpful for you as a beginner if you ever run into problems.

Once you have taken the time to type in the code above into your compiler, you can push on the start button of the compiler in order to get the program to execute and see what will happen.

If you ended up not typing something into the compiler the right way, then you are going to run into trouble that shows up right here. You may get an Output Window type of error. To see what this error is all about, you can just push on it and then make the proper changes to the code so that the compiler is able to read it properly.

Now, if you went through and wrote out the code in the proper way, and the compiler doesn't see that there are other issues with the code, then your code should execute. In this case, a little black window is going to come up on the screen and inside of that box it will say "Hello World". When you see that on the screen and are satisfied with the fact that you are able to write out your own code, and then you can click to exit out of your compiler simply by pressing on your Enter key.

That is all that it takes to write out your first code in the C# programming language!

Chapter 15: How to Code with C++

The next language that we are going to focus on is the C++ coding language. This is a simple programming language to work with and it provides some strong programs that you will love. When compared to the C# language that we learned above, it is a bit easier, but there are still a lot of great programs that you are able to work on. Before we look at any of the syntaxes and codes that you can work with, make sure to download the C++ language onto your computer by visiting the website below: https://www.microsoft.com/en-us/download/details.aspx?id=5555

Creating the Hello World Program

After you download your C++ language and take some time to get used to the environment and how it works, it is time to write out your very first code for this language. We are going to work with the Hello World code so that you get a good idea about how the C++ language works and some of the different parts that come with it. To create your own Hello World program in this coding language, type the following syntax into the compiler:

```
#include <iostream>
using namespace std;

//main() is where program execution begins

int main()
{
        cout <<"Hello World"; //prints Hello World
        return 0;
}
```

After you have taken the time to type this into the compiler, we must take some time to look at the various parts of the code so you know more about what they mean and how you can use them in some of the other codes that you write with this coding language.

The first thing that you need to add into your C++ language is the headers. These headers will hold onto a lot of information about the program so it is important that you don't forget to use them. The header <iostream> will be required for all codes. Next, there is the using namespace std. The point of this is that you are telling the computer which namespace needs to bring up the information that you are looking for.

Then we moved onto the int main() part of the code. This part is responsible for telling the program that this is the primary function where the program needs to start reading and executing. The two slashes that follow are going to be any comments or notes that you would like to leave in the code to help yourself or other programmers who are looking through it. All of these parts then come together in order to help you get the words "Hello World" to print off on your screen.

Comments in the code

We touched on this briefly in the last section, but comments are going to be so important when it comes to working on the C++ language. These comments make it easier to explain what is happening in your code. If another programmer looks through the code and sees this information, they will know that a particular part is going to behave in a certain way. And if you write out the code properly, the compiler will see it and just skip over that information to the next part that it needs to execute. This allows you to leave those little notes without worrying about it messing up the program.

The variables in C++

The variables are important in the C++ coding language because they will help you to name or provide a value for any data that is in your program. Each of these variables will come in a different type, even with the code that we decided to write above. The variable will also be there to help you know the layout and the size of the memory space that is needed for a specific variable and it can hold onto the values that go with that variable inside your memory.

When you decide to name some of your variables in this coding language, you have some choices. You can work with letters, digits, and even an underscore in the name. But make sure that you never use a digit as the beginning of the name. Using the other two characters to start the name of a variable is just fine. You will find that to work with your code, there are actually a variety of variables that you can use. But some of the ones that are the most common include:

- Bool: These variables are in charge of storing values that are either true or false.
- Int: This is going to be the variable that is the natural size of an integer.
- Char: This variable is going to be just one single unit and is often an integer as well.
- Void: This variable is going to be the one that you see if there isn't a type of variable present in your code.

When you work on a code, it is important to declare all of your variables. This makes it easier for the computer to figure out that a variable is present and then it helps the computer know the name and the type before it proceeds through the code. The variable declaration will then have meaning when the compiler gets ahold of it since this is the part that will do all of the heavy lifting when reading through the code. You will find that the extern keyword is a good one to use if you would like to declare your variable, no matter where it is placed inside of the code.

Now, this all may seem a little bit confusing right now if you are not used to working with coding at all in the past. Let's look at how you can write out one of your variables in the C++ language by taking a look at the code that is below:

```
#include <iostream>
using namespace std;

// Variable declaration:
extern int a, b;
extern int c;
extern float f;

int main () {
  // Variable definition:
  int a, b;
  int c;
```

```
float f;

// actual initialization
a = 10;
b = 20;
c = a + b;

cout << c << endl ;

f = 70.0/3.0;
cout << f << endl ;

return 0;
}
```

Take some time to type this code into your compiler and execute it to see what will happen!

Chapter 16: How to Code with Python

The Python coding language is a good one to learn how to use if you have no experience in the world of coding but you want to be able to do some powerful codes and learn quickly. This language was designed to be easy for beginners to learn, but that doesn't mean that you will be disappointed with the codes that you are able to write. Before we take a closer look at all that you are able to do with the help of the Python language, make sure you download the Python language, as well as the right IDE and compiler, onto your computer by visiting www.python.org/downloads.

Variables in Python

Once you have the Python code on your computer, it is time to learn some of the basics of coding in this language. The first step is to learn more about variables. Variables in Python are going to work similarly to what we have talked about in the other coding languages when it comes to Python. With this language, any time you create a new variable, you are reserving some space on the memory to hold it. In some cases, the type of data that is in the variable is able to tell the interpreter to save that memory space, and sometimes it does all the work for you because it will automatically choose where to store this information on the reserved memory.

How to assign values to the variables

All your variables need to be assigned a value in order to work. The value can be almost anything that you like, such as a string of words, a string of numbers, or something similar. A variable in Python doesn't need you to go through the explicit declaration to reserve some space in the memory like you may need to do with other coding languages. This is something that the Python code is able to do on its own any time that you place a value together with a variable. To do this, you just need to have the equals sign between the value and the variable you assign with it. Some good examples of how to do this include the following:

X = 10   #an integer assignment
Pi = 3.14   #a floating point assignment
Y= 200   #an integer assignment
Empname = "Arun Baruah"   #a string assignment

Comments can also come into play when working on a code in Python, just like with the other coding languages. To leave any comment that you want in the code, you just need to work with the (#) sign. This allows you to leave a message, name a code, or do something else inside the code without it messing with the program that you write. The interpreter is not going to read anything that comes after this sign because you just want to leave a note.

The next thing that we are going to work on will often depend on the version of Python that you downloaded. If you choose to go with Python 2, you will need to write out the word print ahead of the information that you want the code to read through. With Python 3, you are required to put the information in parenthesis to make this work.

print("y = %d" %y)
print("x = %d" %x)
print("Employee Name is %s" %empname)

These would then be put through the interpreter and the outputs that you would get should be

X = 10
Y = 200
Employee Name is Arun Baruah

To try this out, open up your Python compiler and type the code in. you will be able to see the answers that we have above as long as you type the code in properly. This is a simple example of how you are able to work with the variables in Python and get the codes to work the way that you need.

Assigning multiple values to a variable

Above we talked about how you can assign a single value to one single variable. This will do a lot in many of your codes, but there are times when you will want to work with multiple assignments. What this means is that you will want to take one value and assign it to two or more variables at once. To do this, you can follow the same idea above but just add in the equal sign in between each of the variables that you want to assign to the same value. You can do these on separate lines if you would like, but you can also just use the equal sign to make things easier and more organized. To do this, you would just need to write out something like a = b = c = 1.

What this tells your compiler is that you want a, b, and c to be tied in with the value of 1 and that they all have the same value when the code runs. This also puts them all in the same location in the memory of your computer to make it easier to pull them up.

Some of the standard types of data

The next thing that we are going to look at in the Python language is the different types of data that you can work with.

These data types are going to be used throughout the code to help you define the operations that you are working on. They also help to explain to others who may look at the code the storage method that is being used based on the type of data. In Python, there are five main types of data that are standard and that you will use often in your coding. These types of data include numbers, strings, lists, dictionary, and tuple.

Number data types are simple because they will just hold onto numeric values. They will be created as an object as soon as you go through and assign a value to them. To take this further, there are also going to be different types of numerics that you can work on including:

- Int: These are the signed integers
- Long: These are the integers that are considered long. They could be called octal or hexadecimal.
- Float: These are the floating point real values
- Complex: These would be any complex numbers.

One thing that you should consider is if you are writing a variable that has numbers and letters inside of it. It is perfectly acceptable to use the lowercase l to do this, but the proper coding practice is going to be to use the uppercase L. This ensures that the l and the 1 don't get mixed up in the code and you don't run into troubles later on since they look so similar to each other.

Strings

In this coding language, the strings are going to be any contiguous set of characters that you will show off with the use of quotation marks. Python makes it easy for you to use either a single or a double quote, but you have to make sure that you keep things consistent throughout when you do it. Therefore, if you start out a string and you use a double quote, then the end needs to be a double quote or you will confuse the compiler. This is the same for the single quotes that you use. Both the double and the single quotes are going to mean the same thing in your code; you just need to make sure that you keep them consistent in the codes you are writing.

You can also have a few options when it comes to telling the compiler which part of the string you want to print. You can use some special characters to do this to make sure that only certain parts of the string show up in the code if you would like. Below are some examples of how you can do this in the compiler.

str = 'Hi Python!'
print(str)   #prints complete string

print(str[0])   #prints the first character of the string

print(str[2:5])   #prints characters starting from the 3rd to the 5th

print(str[2:])#prints string starting from the 3rd character

print(str*2)   #prints the string two times

print(str+"Guys")   #prints concatenated string

What are lists?

When you are working on data types in Python, lists are going to be the most versatile one that you can work on. The list is going to include a lot of different items that will either be separated out with commas or with some square brackets. These are going to be similar to the arrays that you will see in C. The difference here is which items are on the list.

The values that you will put into the list can be accessed with a slice operator or with the : symbol with the indexes starting at 0 at the beginning of your list and then working on down until you end up with -1. Some good examples of how these lists are able to work in the Python language include the following:

list = ['mainu', 'shainu', 86, 3.14, 50.2]

tinylist = [123, 'arun']

print)list)   #prints complete list

print(list[0]) #prints the first element of the list

print(list[1:3]- #prints elements starting from the second element and going to the third

print(list [2:]) #prints all of the elements of the list starting with the 3rd element.

*Print(tinylist*2) #prints the list twice.*

Print(list + tinylist) #prints the concatenated lists.

The importance of keywords in your code

Python is similar to some other coding languages is that it has a few words that are considered keywords. These keywords are going to be any word that is reserved to give commands to the compiler and you shouldn't use them in other places in the code. These words need to just be saved for telling the compiler what it needs to do and if you place them improperly throughout the code, you are going to end up with some issues.

In the most recent version of this language, there are 33 of these reserved words. Some of the ones you need to be careful about include "if, elif, yield, not, del, nonlocal, from, def, true, try, return, or, in, except, and else.) Those are just a few of the keywords. As you work through some of the different codes that you can write with Python, you will quickly start to recognize some more of the keywords that you need to reserve for giving the compiler some commands.

Statements

When you are working on a code in this language, there are going to be a lot of statements and expressions that come up to help the interpreter know what to do. Expressions are there to help you process any objects that are in your code, and often these are going to be embedded inside of the statements that make sure your code can run.

A statement is a simple part of the whole code, but they are still important to work with. These statements are just a unit of code that you can send over to the interpreter so that it can execute what you want. You can write all the code that you want, but if you don't have these statements present in it, you aren't going to get the compiler to do anything that you want.

When you type a statement into the compiler, especially if you are using the interactive mode of the compiler, the interpreter is going to be in charge of executing it. As long as you put in the statement and the other parts of the code properly, you will then see all of the results of that statements how up on the screen. If you are trying to write out many lines to get the code to execute, working with a script that contains a good and easy to read the sequence of these statements can make a big difference. To see how this sequence of statements works, look at the following

```
#All of these are statements
X = 56
Name = "Mainu"
Z = float(X)
Print(X)
Print(Name)
Print(Z)
```

Working with operators and operands

Working with these features of the Python coding language can really add some more power behind the codes you are writing. You need to remember that there is going to be an order of evaluation that is followed. Think back to some of the rules that you had to follow when you were in math class. There were specific signs that had to be taken care of first, or you wouldn't get the right answer when you got started. When working with the operands in Python, the same kind of idea needs to be followed.

When you end up with more than one of the operand types in the code, then you need to use PEMDAS to help you to get started. What this means is that you will work with everything that is in parenthesis first, then the exponents, then multiplication, division, addition, and subtraction to end it all out. If you find that there are several of the same operand, such as two sets of numbers that need to be added together, then you just go from left to right to get it all done. The same way that you did things back when you were in math class will help you to write out these operands when you work on a code.

You should also know a little bit about the modulus operator because it can help in this language. The modulus operator is the one that is going to work with some of the integers that you encounter and it will yield the remainder once the first operand has been divided out by the second one.

Working with the Python coding language can be a lot of fun. It is designed to be easy enough for a beginner to work with, but still has the power that you need to write some amazing codes and programs.

Chapter 17: How to Code with C

The next language that we are going to look at is the C language. This is a simple coding language to learn how to use and you are able to write codes that are any length that you wish, from one line to a long script depending on what your program needs. While it is possible to make some complex codes with the C language, we are going to keep this basic and show you some of the simple things that you can do with this language. Before you get started, you need to download the C language, along with the Visual Studio, which can be found at https://www.visualstudio.com/vs/

Writing out a dummy code in C

The first thing that we need to work on is writing out a dummy code. This isn't going to present you with an output like what we did in the other coding languages, but it at least helps you to learn how to create and then save a code in this language. That can really set you up for success later on.

To work on this dummy code, you need to open up the IDE that you chose to work with in this language. Then you can go and click on the New Button before opening up an Empty

File. We are going to type in a code to this IDE so that it is created and then we can save it. To keep things simple, just type in the following to get started:

main() {}

Now that we have a code written, it is time to learn how to save this file for later. To do this, you simply need to click on the Save button that is located in your IDE. This will make it so that the code saves either on the default of your computer (which it will do if you make no other selections), or you can choose where you want the code to save. Either way, make sure that you remember where the file is saved so it is easier to find it later.

While saving that file, not only is its location important, but you need to give it a name that is easy to remember. You don't want to end up saving a bunch of codes and then having no clue which one goes to what. For this example, we are going to give the file the name "dummy.c". Once this source code is created and saved to the computer, we need to click on the button that says Build.

For this example, the code that we are trying to build is not going to work. What you will see here is the minimum of the C program, or the dummy that we talked about above. All of the codes that you create in C will need the main function because this is the source of executing the program in this language. The curly brackets are going to hold onto the main function for the code.

Since the code that we just worked on is a dummy source code, and one that we are simply experimenting on a bit, we didn't take the time to add in any curly brackets to it. When you add this to your compiler and try to get it to execute, you will end up with no output simply because we didn't add anything into the curly brackets. As you get more familiar with the C language, you can always add in something to that part and expand out the dummy code to make it work for your needs.

At this point, you have technically written out your very first code with the C programming language. While you didn't really get an output with what we have in the code right now, you still completed this part of the code properly. Of course, this is a basic form of writing codes in this language, and you can always add in so much more to make it more powerful and make it work better and actually create a program. Some of the basic things that you may want to add into the code will include things like the keywords, functions, operators, structure, values, and variables.

Working on your second code

Now that you understand a little bit of the parts that come with the C language code, it is time to work on that dummy code a bit more and expand on it to get something a bit stronger. To get started, you need to bring out the dummy.c program that we created earlier. Then we are going to work to make the main function an integer function. What this means is that we are going to change the code so that it provides you with an integer value as the return in your operating system. We will take the dummy.c program and do a bit of editing to make this work.

Once you have the dummy.c program up, you can work inside the editor in order to place the "int" keyword before the "main" part. This ensures that you will get an output that is an integer. Also, make sure that there is a space that occurs between the keywords so that the compiler can read them a little bit better.

This is just the first step that we are going to write out. It is the same that we had in our dummy program, but it has an extra part to it. Now we need to go a bit further and add in a statement to this main function. This will ensure that our program is going to provide an output on the screen. We are going to do this by adding in the number three for the output.

Computer Programming

To do this, we need to make sure that the return keyword is used in the code. An example of the kind of syntax that you would use with this one includes the following:

int main()
{
    return(3);
}

One thing to note here is that your statement must have semicolons at the end. From here, you need to go through and save the file before hitting the button to Build. As long as the code above is written into your compiler properly, you should be able to click the Run button and end up with a value of 3 that shows up on the screen.

Any time that you are working with that original dummy program and you want to add in some output, you must make sure that you use the output function. The keywords in the C language are important, but if you add them into the code all on their own, then they are not going to provide you with an output on the screen. You are able to get things to print up on the screen if you simply use the "puts" command in the right place in the code. A good example of how to write this kind of thing out includes:

```
int main()
{
        puts("I am the King of the C programming world");
            return 3;
}
```

When you go through and save this particular code and click on the Build button. At this point, there is going to be a warning or an error that comes up on the screen. In some cases, this may not show up, but there is still another step that needs to be done here. Before the puts function is able to work, you must make sure that there is a definition that is put inside so that the compiler knows what to do. The definition that is in here and used for the puts will be in the I/O header file and this needs to be placed into your source code using a preprocessor directive to get the work done.

To help you see how this is going to work, the following syntax is going to make it easier to understand:

```
#include<stdio.h>

int main()
{
        puts("I am the King of the C programming world");
            return 3;
```

}

This syntax is a good one to use because it has the preprocessor directive inside of it along with the definition that you need for your puts function. From here, you will be able to save that file before building and running the code. If you typed all the information into the compiler properly, you won't have any errors come up and you will see the value three come up on the screen. And it is as simple as that to take your dummy code and turn it into a code that provides an output when working with the C language.

Chapter 18: How to Code with JavaScript

If you are interested in writing out some codes that can be used online or on a website, then you need to learn how to work with JavaScript. This one works well with Java and there are some similarities that can come up between the two of them. This language is easy to learn and it definitely one that you will want to work with if you plan to do any kind of coding for online use.

Before you get started with the JavaScript language, you need to download the language. You can find this at www.javascript.com/download.htm. JavaScript is a versatile coding language that you are able to inject anywhere you would like in your page. As long as you have the HTML tags <script>...</script> around what you would like to insert. However, in most cases, you will be recommended to place the script that you want to use in between the head sections or the <head>...</head> tags.

When the browser is looking at the content on the page or the HTML on the page, it is just going to read the whole thing like reading through a book. However, when the browser program comes to the <script> tag, it will start to interpret whatever you have written between these tags and won't stop until it reaches the </script> part of the tag. This allows the program to interpret what you would like to have on the page in any location that you would like.

Writing your first program

Let's dive right into the JavaScript code and look at how you can write out some of your own codes in this language. First, you will want to open up an html file and then you can write out a simple (or complex), program with the help of JavaScript. We are going to use the following syntax to help us get started:

<!DOCTYPE html>
<html>
<head>
<meta charset- "ISO-8859-1">
<title> My First JavaScript Program </title>
</head>
<body>
   <script language = "javascript" type = "text/javascript">
      document.write("Welcome to my JavaScript First Program");
   </script>

```
</body>
</html>
```

If you are new to programming, this may look like a lot. However, it is actually simple. When you type this into your JavaScript compiler, you are going to get the sentence "Welcome to JavaScript First Program" to come up on your screen.

If you want with the code above, you could leave out all the spaces. Line breaks and spaces are not important in the JavaScript code, which makes it a little bit different from some of the other coding languages. The compiler will read it all whether there are spaces there are not. We add in the spaces because it makes the code much easier for the programmer to look through, but if you miss a space or a line break, then this is not such a big deal with this language.

However, when it comes to the use of semicolons, you will want to add this after all of your statements. If the statements are all on different lines, then you can choose, but it is often considered good coding practice to add these in to make things look better. If you decide to write out the code in a continuous line, then you must add in these semicolons or you will confuse the compiler.

Another thing to consider is that the JavaScript language is going to be sensitive to the cases that you use. This means that the way that you use the cases in this language needs to consistent the whole time. Whether you are labeling your functions or identifiers, naming variables and keywords, or anything else. When working in JavaScript, the words learn and LEARN and Learn will all be seen differently so be careful with the case that you use.

It is also possible for you to write out comments in JavaScript. If you write a single line comment, you will simply use a double slash to comment it out in your code. If the comment that you want to write out is a little bit longer, you would ad the /* at the beginning of the comment and then the */ when the comment is done and you want the compiler to start reading through the code again. You can write out as many of these comments as you would like, but try to limit them as much as possible so that the code doesn't become too cluttered and hard to read through.

Conclusion

Thank you for making it through to the end of *Hacking and Programming*. Let's hope it was informative and able to provide you with all of the tools you need to achieve your goals whatever they may be.

The next step is to put some of this new knowledge to the test. We have spent some time talking about some of the best hacking practices to help protect your computer and your computer network as well as some of the biggest threats and how to watch out for them. We also talked about a variety of coding languages that you as a beginner can get started with and even some examples of how you would write codes in each one. For someone who is looking to get a good understanding of many basic technology ideas and processes, this guidebook has everything that you need!

Finally, if you found this book useful in any way, a review on Amazon is always appreciated!

Computer Programming

On the go?

Get the audio version of this book for FREE when you sign up for a free Audible trial!

CLICK/TAP HERE

For UK Version GO HERE

Made in the USA
Columbia, SC
18 October 2018